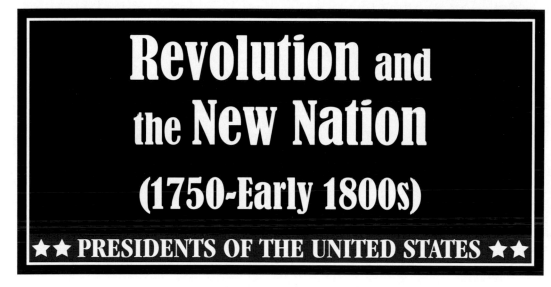

Revolution and the New Nation (1750-Early 1800s)

★★ PRESIDENTS OF THE UNITED STATES ★★

By Marcia Amidon Lusted

WEIGL PUBLISHERS INC.

Published by Weigl Publishers Inc.
350 5th Avenue, Suite 3304 PMB 6G
New York, NY 10118-0069
Website: www.weigl.com

Library of Congress Cataloging-in-Publication Data

Lüsted, Marcia Amidon.
  Revolution and the new nation / Marcia Amidon Lüsted.
     p. cm. -- (Presidents of the United States)
  Includes bibliographical references and index.
  ISBN 978-1-59036-739-1 (hard cover : alk. paper) -- ISBN 978-1-59036-740-7 (soft cover : alk. paper) 1.
Presidents--United States--History--18th century--Juvenile literature. 2. Presidents--United States--History--19th
century--Juvenile literature. 3. United States--Politics and government--1789-1815--Juvenile literature. 4.
United States--Politics and government--1815-1861--Juvenile literature. 5. Washington, George, 1732-1799--
Juvenile literature. 6. Adams, John, 1735-1826--Juvenile literature. 7. Jefferson, Thomas, 1743-1826--Juvenile
literature. 8. Madison, James, 1751-1836--Juvenile literature. 9. Monroe, James, 1758-1831--Juvenile literature.
10. United States--History--1783-1865--Juvenile literature. I. Title.
  E176.1.L93 2006
  973.4092'2--dc22
  [B]

                                        2007012643

Printed in the United States of America
1 2 3 4 5 6 7 8 9 0 11 10 09 08 07

Project Coordinator
Heather C. Hudak

Design
Terry Paulhus

Photo Credits: Historic Print & Map Company: page 15.

Contents

United States Presidents

REVOLUTION AND THE NEW NATION (1750–EARLY 1800s)

George Washington
(1789–1797)

John Adams
(1797–1801)

Thomas Jefferson
(1801–1809)

James Madison
(1809–1817)

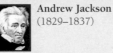
James Monroe
(1817–1825)

EXPANSION AND REFORM (EARLY 1800s–1861)

John Quincy Adams
(1825–1829)

Andrew Jackson
(1829–1837)

Martin Van Buren
(1837–1841)

William Henry Harrison
(1841)

John Tyler
(1841–1845)

James Polk
(1845–1849)

Zachary Taylor
(1849–1850)

Millard Fillmore
(1850–1853)

Franklin Pierce
(1853–1857)

James Buchanan
(1857–1861)

CIVIL WAR AND RECONSTRUCTION (1850–1877)

Abraham Lincoln
(1861–1865)

Andrew Johnson
(1865–1869)

Ulysses S. Grant
(1869–1877)

DEVELOPMENT OF THE INDUSTRIAL UNITED STATES (1870–1900)

Rutherford B. Hayes
(1877–1881)

James Garfield
(1881)

Chester Arthur
(1881–1885)

Grover Cleveland
(1885–1889)
(1893–1897)

Benjamin Harrison
(1889–1893)

William McKinley
(1897–1901)

THE EMERGENCE OF MODERN AMERICA (1890–1930)

Theodore Roosevelt
(1901–1909)

William H. Taft
(1909–1913)

Woodrow Wilson
(1913–1921)

Warren Harding
(1921–1923)

Calvin Coolidge
(1923–1929)

THE GREAT DEPRESSION AND WORLD WAR II (1929–1945)

Herbert Hoover
(1929–1933)

Franklin D. Roosevelt
(1933–1945)

POST-WAR UNITED STATES (1945–EARLY 1970s)

Harry S. Truman
(1945–1953)

Dwight Eisenhower
(1953–1961)

John F. Kennedy
(1961–1963)

Lyndon Johnson
(1963–1969)

CONTEMPORARY UNITED STATES (1968 TO THE PRESENT)

Richard Nixon
(1969–1974)

Gerald Ford
(1974–1977)

Jimmy Carter
(1977–1981)

Ronald Reagan
(1981–1989)

George H. W. Bush
(1989–1993)

William J. Clinton
(1993–2001)

George W. Bush
(2001–)

Revolution and the New Nation

John Cabot set sail from Bristol, England, for North America in 1497. He landed in Newfoundland and was the first person to explore North America.

America in 1750 was poised on the edge of great change. Not yet a country, it consisted of 13 colonies clustered along the coast of the Atlantic Ocean. These colonies were under the rule of Great Britain, which had sent its first explorers to the lands of North America in 1497.

By 1760, British King George III had control over the colonies and the 1.6 million people who lived there. Americans, however, were rebelling against British rule. They felt they were not given the same rights as British citizens. Few British officials had ever visited the new land of America. They did not understand the country or its people. Americans felt that the time had come to rule themselves. The British did not think the Americans were capable of being independent. William Pitt, a British statesman, wrote, "This is the mother country, they are the children; they must obey, and we prescribe."

The 13 colonies were not a unified group. They were a collection of settlements with different needs and opinions. In the early days of colonial America, farmers built large plantations in the southern colonies. These plantations grew tobacco, cotton, and rice. Plantations required a great deal of labor, and their owners relied on slaves. Slaves were brought from Africa to work. Slaves could be used in trade. For example, a colonial ship captain might trade a load of fish for British guns and cloth. The captain could then trade the guns and cloth for slaves. Many colonial merchants became wealthy by trading slaves. They did not want to see slavery outlawed. Other Americans felt that slavery was wrong.

In the Revolutionary War of 1775-1783, America fought to free itself from British rule and become a country of its own. During this time, many people played important roles in shaping the future of the United States. Some of them are known as the Founding Fathers because they helped to create the new government. They include the 39 men who signed the United States of America's Constitution in 1787 and the first men to hold the title of president of the United States. George Washington, John Adams, Thomas Jefferson, James Madison, and James Monroe were responsible for establishing much of the government as it exists today.

Records show that the first slaves were brought from Africa to America in 1619.

George Washington's Early Years

When most people think of the title "Father of Our Country," they think of George Washington. He was one of the most important figures in the Revolutionary War and during the early years of the United States of America.

George Washington was born in Virginia on February 22, 1732. His father, Augustine Washington, owned several plantations. When he died in 1743, he left 10,000 acres of land and 50 slaves to his family.

George's education began in a one-room schoolhouse. There, he learned the basics of reading, writing, and mathematics, as well as good manners. He hoped to attend school in Great Britain like his older half-brothers Lawrence and Augustine, Jr. After the death of their father when George was 11 years old, Lawrence became a mentor to him. Lawrence took George hunting and fishing and helped him with his studies.

At the age of 14, George wanted to join the British Navy, but his mother refused to give him permission. George finished school at the age of 15. He was good at mathematics and art, and he became interested in surveying. Lawrence introduced George to his father-in-law, Colonel William Fairfax, one of the wealthiest landowners in Virginia. George went with Fairfax to survey his properties in the Shenandoah Valley. From 1749 until 1751, George was the official land surveyor for Culpeper County, Virginia. Lawrence died in 1752. Soon after, George inherited the Mount Vernon estate, which had passed from his father to his brother, and he became a plantation owner.

> "The time is near at hand which must determine whether Americans are to be free men or slaves."
>
> *George Washington*

George Washington lived and was buried at his estate, Mount Vernon, near Alexandria, Virginia.

In 1752, Washington became a major in the Virginia **militia**. Governor Robert Dinwiddie sent him to the frontier near Lake Erie. Washington's mission was to warn the French not to occupy lands that had been claimed by the British. The French rejected this warning. Over the next several years, Washington would have many more confrontations with the French and their American Indian allies. These battles led to the French and Indian War from 1754 to 1763. In 1755, Washington became the commander of the Virginia militia. He served until 1758, when he returned to tobacco farming.

On January 6, 1759, Washington married Martha Dandridge Custis. She was a widow with two children from her first marriage. Washington became a father to her son, John, and her daughter, Martha. Later, Washington cared for Martha's grandchildren and his many nieces and nephews.

Upon returning home, Washington became interested in politics. He was elected to the Virginia House of Burgesses. The Virginia House of Burgesses was the first American government that allowed the people to elect their leaders. Originally, its members could pass laws until the British began to restrict its powers. As a member, Washington began to protest some of the British colonial policies. These protests would one day lead him to become the first U.S. president.

George Washington read to his troops at a Sunday morning church service during the French and Indian War.

The Path to War

Most members of the Virginia House of Burgesses were planters. These men owned large plantations and were wealthy and educated. They had the time to participate in politics, and they saw political leadership as a birthright. Someone who was not born in this social class rarely achieved political power.

As a member of the Virginia House of Burgesses, Washington spoke out against many of the policies that the British were enforcing in the colonies. The Royal Proclamation of 1763 discouraged settlement in the West, where Washington owned land. In 1765, the British enacted the Stamp Act. This taxation of all printed items led to an unexpected response among the colonists. People rioted and hung dummies dressed as tax collectors from lampposts. The Virginia House of Burgesses protested the Stamp Act by issuing the Stamp Tax Resolves. In the resolves, the burgesses proclaimed that only elected representatives of the colonists had the right to tax them. The British colonial governor was so angry at the Virginia House of Burgesses that he had them officially **disbanded**. The burgesses continued to meet in secrecy. Washington became an important leader in their resistance of unfair British rule.

> **"I will raise one thousand men, subsist them at my own expense, and march myself at their head for the relief of Boston."**
>
> *George Washington, speaking at the First Continental Congress, 1774*

An angry mob rioted in the streets of New York to protest the Stamp Act.

The Stamp Act was **repealed** in 1766, but the British continued to impose other taxes on the colonists. The Townshend Acts of 1767 placed a tax on tea, a beverage most colonists drank every day. These acts led to the Boston Tea Party, when colonists dumped a cargo of tea into the harbor.

In response to the tea party, the British closed Boston Harbor and sent soldiers to occupy the city. Since no ships could enter or leave the harbor, many citizens of Boston were unable to work. They began to worry about starving. This unified the colonists by making them more sympathetic to Boston and to each other.

The colonists formed Committees of Correspondence. These were groups of citizens in different colonies who would write back and forth to exchange news. These committees were a way to keep the colonies in touch with each other.

The Committees of Correspondence decided to meet in person. They became **delegates** to the First Continental Congress held in Philadelphia in 1774. Every colony except for Georgia sent delegates. Washington represented Virginia. The Congress issued a Declaration of Rights and Grievances addressed to King George III. They wanted to be fairly treated by the British. They threatened to retaliate against any more unfair taxes or policies by cutting off all trade between the American colonies and the British. Washington offered to lead men to Boston and fight the British occupation.

The British declared the Continental Congress an illegal assembly and refused to consider the list of grievances. Left with no other options, the colonists began to make preparations for war.

The Sons of Liberty threw chests of tea into Boston Harbor to protest the tax on tea.

THE BOSTON TEA PARTY

When a tax was placed on tea, the colonists quickly boycotted British tea. They had tea from other countries smuggled into the United States. In 1774, the British shipped millions of pounds of unwanted tea to the colonies. Some colonial ports turned the ships back, not allowing the cargo to be unloaded. One city left the tea to rot on the docks. When the royal governor would not send back the tea in Boston Harbor, about 50 colonists from an organization called the Sons of Liberty boarded the ship and dumped the tea into the harbor. This act of rebellion became known as the Boston Tea Party.

Washington as Commander in Chief

At the meeting of the Second Continental Congress in 1775, the delegates agreed that the time had come to fight back against the British. They decided to raise a volunteer army from every colony. They needed someone to serve as the commander in chief of this Continental Army. The Congress unanimously chose George Washington.

> "Liberty, when it begins to take root, is a plant of rapid growth."
> *George Washington*

Washington agreed to serve as the commander in chief, but he refused to accept pay for his position. Washington traveled to Cambridge, Massachusetts, and took command of his army on July 3, 1775. This army consisted of volunteers who were mostly rough, untrained men with few weapons. Under Washington's leadership, they successfully forced the British to evacuate Boston in 1776.

Washington's army suffered three defeats at the battles of Long Island, Manhattan, and White Plains before they retreated into New Jersey and Pennsylvania. After crossing the Delaware River, they defeated the British at Trenton, New Jersey.

The army spent the winter of 1777 in Valley Forge, Pennsylvania, where living conditions were harsh. That winter, 2,000 men died of cold, disease, and starvation. By this time, Washington's army was disciplined and well-trained. They went on to defeat the British with the help of

Washington's troops camped at Valley Forge, Pennsylvania, during the winter of 1777. Many men died of cold, starvation, and disease.

the French army. On October 19, 1781, British general Cornwallis surrendered. America had won its independence.

With the defeat of the British, the new country needed to form a permanent government. The colonists were not in complete agreement about what this government should be like. In 1783, Washington prevented a mutiny by senior officers who wanted to disband the Continental Congress. Some people wanted to name Washington king of America. Washington insisted on preserving a **democracy**, where the people had a voice in the affairs of the country.

Washington was now one of the most influential political figures in the country, but he was not seeking a career in public service. He resigned from the army in December 1783, and retired to Mount Vernon. In 1787, state leaders met in Philadelphia to revise the federal government. This meeting became known as the Constitutional Convention.

At first, Washington refused to attend, but at the urging of state leaders, he presided over the Convention. Although Washington hoped to retire from politics, he was elected the first president of the United States on February 4, 1789. He is the only president in history to be elected unanimously. Washington would have an even greater role to play as president than he did as commander of the American army.

Washington was sworn in as the first president of the United States at Federal Hall in New York City.

WASHINGTON BECOMES PRESIDENT

On April 16, 1789, George Washington left Mount Vernon for New York City, which was the federal capital. His journey covered nearly half of the United States as it was at that time. Everywhere he went, towns threw huge celebrations in his honor.

Washington took the oath of office as president on April 30, 1789. Crowds in the street cheered and applauded. New York Chancellor Robert R. Livingston administered the oath. Then, he turned to the crowd and shouted, "Long live George Washington, president of the United States!"

Washington's Presidency

Washington was the first president of the United States. He had no examples to follow, and it would be up to him to establish the **precedents** of behavior and action that every other president would follow.

Washington wanted the office of president to be one of dignity and respect. At the same time, he wanted to avoid the kinds of ceremonies that would remind people of royal courts. His careful attention to appearance and behavior gave the office of president the proper degree of respectability.

Washington's **cabinet** consisted of a secretary of state, a secretary of treasury, and a secretary of war. These men would be his closest advisors and oversee some of the most important parts of the government.

As well as establishing the office of president, Washington was involved in many other important acts. These acts were laws that created some of the most vital parts of the new government. In 1789, the Judiciary Act established 13 district courts, one for each state, and three circuit courts to hear appeals from these state courts. The U.S. Supreme Court had the power to make final decisions over all of these lower courts. In this way, Washington made certain that national institutions had the final authority over state institutions.

The Residence Act of 1792 stated that the federal government would move to a new permanent city to be constructed on the Potomac River. Washington would choose the city's specific location and appoint three commissioners to oversee its design and construction. After his death, this city would be given Washington's name. This city is present-day Washington, D.C.

George Washington became the first president of the United States on April 30, 1789.

Under Washington's leadership, the government established the Bank Act of 1791 and the Coinage Act of 1792. The first founded a national bank with the power to make loans and handle government funds. The Coinage Act established a national mint to make coins and fixed the values for gold, silver, and copper coins.

George Washington retired in 1796 after his second term as president. He died on December 14, 1799. Remembered as a national hero, he left the United States a legacy of freedom from British rule and helped to establish a strong national government. One of his officers, Henry Lee, said it best in his eulogy for Washington: "First in war, first in peace, and first in the hearts of his countrymen."

> **"I walk on untrodden ground. There is scarcely any part of my conduct which may not hereafter be drawn into precedent."**
>
> *George Washington, in a letter dated January 9, 1790*

This historical map from 1793 shows the plans for the city of Washington, D.C.

John Adams' Early Years

The man who would become the second president of the United States was born in the town of Braintree, Massachusetts, on October 30, 1735. As a child, John Adams was only interested in being a farmer, even though his father wanted him to attend Harvard and become a minister.

Adams graduated from Harvard College in 1755. After graduating, he taught school in Worcester, Massachusetts for a few years. Instead of becoming a minister, he chose to become a lawyer. He felt that becoming a minister would threaten his "liberty to think" because he would have to change his opinions to match those of the church.

> **"I must think myself independent as long as I live. The feeling is essential to my existence."** *John Adams*

In 1758, Adams returned to Braintree to start his own law practice. He began courting a woman named Abigail Smith. Abigail was an intelligent, well-educated woman from a wealthy family. John and Abigail were married by her father, a minister, in 1764.

For several years, Abigail and John moved their household between Braintree and Boston to meet the demands of John's law practice and the circuit court system. This system required him to travel from court to court in order to conduct business. Abigail was often left at home to manage their farm and raise their five children.

Later, Adams would travel as part of his political career. Abigail wrote long and frequent letters to him of support and guidance. They have been preserved as important records of their lives and of the early years of the United States.

John Adams was the second president of the United States.

Adams often took on **controversial** cases in his role as a lawyer. In 1770, nine British soldiers were charged with the murders of five colonists during a street riot. This event became known as the Boston Massacre. Adams defended these soldiers in court. He believed that everyone had the right to a fair trial, even though most people wanted to blame the British for the massacre. Adams argued that the British soldiers had been defending themselves against an angry mob. As a result of his arguments, the judge found six soldiers not guilty. Two of the soldiers were found guilty of manslaughter, a lesser charge than murder.

Adam's successful defense of the British soldiers did not mean that he supported British rule over the colonies. He would become one of the key figures in the American Revolution.

On March 5, 1770, angry colonists confronted British soldiers in Boston, Massachusetts. Five colonists died when the British opened fire. John Adams helped defend the British soldiers, saying that they had been provoked by the mob.

Adams' Early Political Career

Along with Washington, Adams led the opposition to the Stamp Act of 1765 and supported the Boston Tea Party. After the British closed the port of Boston, he felt that the colonists had no choice but to fight for their independence.

Adams became a delegate to the First Continental Congress in Philadelphia in 1774. He would eventually serve on 50 different colonial committees working towards independence. His participation earned him the nickname "The Atlas of Independence."

Adams was a delegate to the Second Continental Congress in 1775. He was in charge of the committee that drafted a declaration of independence from Great Britain. While Thomas Jefferson is given the credit for writing the declaration, Adams claimed that he played a key role in the discussions. Later, Adams would regret not writing the Declaration of Independence himself, claiming that "Jefferson ran away with…all the glory of it."

> "The die is cast. Swim or sink, live or die, survive or perish with my country was my unalterable determination." *John Adams*

Members of the First Continental Congress, including John Adams, watched as John Hancock became the first person to sign the Declaration of Independence.

John Adams was sworn in as the first vice president of the United States in 1789, along with President George Washington.

In 1778, Adams was appointed as a joint commissioner to France along with Benjamin Franklin and Arthur Lee. This mission helped **negotiate** the end of the Revolutionary War and enlisted France's aid against the British. He returned to Braintree in the summer of 1779 to represent his town at a convention where a state constitution would be written. The Massachusetts State Constitution, drafted by Adams in 1780, is the oldest constitution in the world still in effect.

Adams helped to negotiate a **treaty** with Great Britain in 1781 and 1782, ending the war. He served as a political minister to Great Britain, returning home to Braintree in 1788. In the election of 1789, Adams received the second-highest number of votes. This made him vice president under George Washington. Adams played a major role in setting up the procedures for the new Senate and cast the deciding vote in legislative measures in the case of a tie.

Adams was the first choice of Washington to run for president in the election of 1796. He defeated Thomas Jefferson, who became Adams' vice president. Although these two men had once been friends, their differing political beliefs had come between them. Adams was a Federalist, and Jefferson, a Republican.

FEDERALISTS VS. REPUBLICANS

Today's political parties have their roots in the first two political factions, the Federalists and the Republicans. During Washington's presidency, two different theories of government developed. The Democratic-Republicans, often referred to as Republicans, believed that political power should remain in the hands of the people. This would keep them from being oppressed by a powerful central government. The Federalists believed in a strong central government run by aristocratic leaders who had the time and talents to run the country. Over time, these two factions would become the two major political parties of today.

Adams' Presidency

John Adams became president in 1797, after one of the most orderly transfers of power in history. He kept all of George Washington's cabinet members. Like Washington, he tried to avoid favoring either political faction, even though he was a member of the Federalist Party.

Adams was determined that the United States would remain neutral with France and Great Britain, who were at war. France had aided the United States during the Revolutionary War, but by 1797, they were refusing to meet with American representatives, and French ships were harassing American ships at sea. In response to France's actions, Adams created the Department of the Navy and began to build up naval forces to combat the French Navy. One of the ships constructed around this time, the U.S.S. *Constitution*, is still intact and is in working order.

The Federalist-controlled Congress wanted the United States to go to war with France. In anticipation of war, they passed the Alien and Sedition Acts. The Alien Act made it difficult for people from other countries to become U.S. citizens. These acts gave the president the power to throw anyone out of the country for any reason. The Sedition Act made it illegal to criticize the government. This was in direct violation of the freedom of speech guaranteed by the U.S. Constitution. The Sedition Act was used to arrest many newspaper editors who spoke out against Federalist policies. The U.S. Supreme Court at this time did not have the power to declare these acts **unconstitutional**. Instead, several states passed resolutions refusing to enforce the acts.

The U.S.S. *Constitution,* also nicknamed "Old Ironsides," was built in the late 1790s and served as a warship in the War of 1812.

Despite popular support for a war against France, Adams began to have second thoughts. A war would be costly, and he was not sure if the United States was prepared for another war. Adams decided that it was best for the country to seek a diplomatic solution by sending a peace mission to France. France agreed to talk to a new U.S. diplomat, and the two countries negotiated a peace agreement.

His decision to negotiate peace with France, and the unpopular Alien and Sedition Acts, caused Adams to lose the presidential election of 1800 to Thomas Jefferson. Adams refused to participate in the festivities for the **inauguration** of Jefferson.

Despite being political enemies, the two men renewed their friendship after they retired from political office. They exchanged letters about the events that had shaped the nation, as well as their political disagreements and their hopes for the country. By coincidence, both men died on July 4, 1826, on the 50-year anniversary of the signing of the Declaration of Independence.

> "When the people have chosen their presidents, they ought to expect that they will act their own independent judgments."
>
> *John Adams*

President John Adams avoided a war with France in the late 1790s.

Adams' Legacy

John Adams is still considered one of the best political philosophers of his time. His achievements include his roles as a leading patriot of the American Revolution and as one of the Founding Fathers of the United States of America. His sense of justice allowed him to successfully defend British soldiers involved in the Boston Massacre. Adams believed in doing what was right.

> **"Our obligations to our country never cease but with our lives."**
>
> *John Adams*

Adams had a primary role in the drafting of the Declaration of Independence, and he persuaded the delegates of the Second Continental Congress to sign the Declaration. The men who signed this document were committing treason against Great Britain and could be put to death. Adams served as a valued diplomat to both Great Britain and France and as the nation's first vice president and second president.

Adams once suggested that his gravestone should read, "Here lies John Adams, who took upon himself the responsibility of the peace with France, in the year 1800." He wished to be remembered for preventing a war with France at a time when the United States was defining itself as a country.

John Adams is remembered as one of the Founding Fathers of the United States of America.

Adams' political philosophies greatly influenced the way the current U.S. government runs.

Adams' political philosophies helped create the strong national government of the United States. While he was serving as political minister to Great Britain in 1787, John Adams wrote the book *A Defense of the Constitutions of Government of the United States of America*. In this book, he called for a balanced government that would equally represent the interests of all people. Working-class citizens would be represented in the lower house of the legislature. Wealthy men would serve in the upper house. A chief executive would act like a king and balance the interests of the other two groups. Today's U.S. government acts in much the same way as Adams' book described.

After losing the election of 1800 to Thomas Jefferson, Adams retired to Braintree, which was now called Quincy. He lived there for the rest of his life, and he witnessed his son, John Quincy Adams, be elected as the sixth president of the United States.

THE WHITE HOUSE

John Adams was the first president to occupy the new executive mansion in Washington. This residency would later be called the White House. When Adams and his family moved in on November 1, 1800, the outside of the mansion was completed, but the interior was still under construction. The plaster walls were wet, the main staircase had not been built, and much of the flooring was unfinished. After his first night in the White House, Adams wrote "I pray heaven to bestow the best blessings on this house and on all that shall hereafter inhabit it. May none but honest and wise men ever rule under this roof."

Thomas Jefferson's Early Years

Thomas Jefferson was one of the most intellectual people to hold the office of president of the United States. He served as the third president, but he was also an ambassador, scientist, writer, planter, and architect.

Jefferson was born on his father's plantation, Shadwell, in Virginia, on April 13, 1743. His father was a planter and politician. His mother was a member of an elite planter family, the Randolphs.

The region where Thomas Jefferson grew up was sparsely populated and had no public education. He went to boarding school. Thomas loved reading and science and learned to play the violin.

When Jefferson was 14, his father died. Three years later, Jefferson decided to further his education and entered the College of William and Mary in Williamsburg, Virginia. Graduating in 1762, Jefferson then trained to be a lawyer and was admitted to the Virginia Bar in 1767.

Jefferson married Martha Wayles Skelton, a young, wealthy widow, in 1772. He brought her to his new home, which was still under construction. The house sat on a hilltop near his father's plantation. He designed his home himself and named it Monticello. Thomas and Martha would have six children, but only one daughter would outlive both of her parents. Martha died in 1782, at 33 years of age.

Thomas Jefferson served as president of the United States from 1801 to 1809.

Jefferson was elected to the Virginia House of Burgesses in 1769. He was not a strong public speaker, like many of the other members, but he was good at writing. As a member of the Virginia House of Burgesses, Jefferson helped to create the Committees of Correspondence as a method for keeping the 13 colonies in touch with each other. He was a member of this committee and wrote many letters to other colonists to share ideas, spread news, and discuss strategies for resisting British policies.

The Virginia House of Burgesses adopted the resolution that would result in the meeting of the First Continental Congress in 1774. Jefferson attended this first Congress and the Second Continental Congress in 1775. At the second Congress, delegates resolved to issue a declaration of independence from Great Britain. Jefferson drafted the declaration and considered it to be the greatest achievement of his life.

Jefferson was elected the governor of Virginia in 1779 and served until 1781. As governor, he struggled to defend Virginia against the British in the Revolutionary War.

THE DECLARATION OF INDEPENDENCE

"We hold these truths to be self-evident, that all men are created equal, that they are endowed by their creator with certain inalienable rights, that among these are life, liberty, and the pursuit of happiness."

Thomas Jefferson wrote these words, from the opening paragraphs of the Declaration of Independence, in the parlor of his lodging house in June 1776. They would form the core beliefs of the U.S. government. They were also a declaration to the British government that the colonies wished to be independent from British rule. The Second Continental Congress approved this declaration on July 4, 1776, a date now celebrated as the birth of the United States of America.

Thomas Jefferson and four other men formed the Declaration Committee during the First Continental Congress in 1774 to prepare a declaration of freedom from British rule. Jefferson is credited with drafting the Declaration of Independence.

Jefferson's Early Political Career

I n 1784, three men set off for Paris, France, as representatives of the new U.S. government. John Adams, Benjamin Franklin, and Thomas Jefferson would be responsible for negotiating commercial treaties with European nations. Jefferson was named the new political minister to France when Franklin retired in 1785.

Jefferson's first role as a diplomat was to create treaties with government officials and private bankers. He often had to answer hostile questions about the United States' finances and stability. Jefferson succeeded in his role, and he became sympathetic to the French in their war with Great Britain.

Jefferson sailed for home in 1789 to become George Washington's secretary of state. He took the oath of office in 1790. When Congress accepted the new U.S. Constitution, Jefferson urged them to adopt the Bill of Rights. The Bill of Rights was the first 10 **amendments** to the Constitution that outlined citizens' basic rights.

Jefferson frequently clashed with Alexander Hamilton, Washington's secretary of treasury. Both Jefferson and Hamilton wanted the United

> "A Bill of Rights is what the people are entitled to against every government, and what no just government should refuse, or rest on inference."
>
> *Thomas Jefferson*

Thomas Jefferson (left) served as President Washington's (right) secretary of state, and Alexander Hamilton (middle) served as Washington's secretary of treasury.

States to remain neutral in the war between Great Britain and France. However, they were partial to different countries. Hamilton was sympathetic to Great Britain, and Jefferson to France.

Their political beliefs concerning the role of the federal government led to the division of the government. Hamilton supported a strong federal government, while Jefferson wanted the state governments to have more power. The ideals of these two men would lead to the creation of the Federalist and Republican parties. Jefferson resigned from Washington's cabinet in 1793 and helped to form the Republican Party.

Jefferson ran for president in 1796, against John Adams. He lost and became vice president instead. As vice president, one of Jefferson's duties was to preside over the U.S. Senate. There were no guidelines for procedures, so Jefferson wrote a manual on parliamentary practice in the U.S. Senate. The rules in this manual are used to run the Senate today.

Jefferson ran for president again in 1800, and this time, he and his opponent, Aaron Burr, tied in the voting of the electoral college. The U.S. House of Representatives voted to decide who would be the president. On the 36th round of votes, Jefferson was elected, and he became the nation's third president. This was the first time that presidential power had transferred from one political party to another.

Jefferson insisted on a simple inauguration. He walked to the Capitol instead of riding in the presidential carriage. After taking the oath of office as president, he assured his opponents that political parties would not divide the government. He told them, "We are all Republicans, we are all Federalists."

Alexander Hamilton served as a delegate to the Constitutional Convention and as the first secretary of treasury.

ALEXANDER HAMILTON

Alexander Hamilton, George Washington's secretary of treasury, helped create the United States' two political parties. He believed in a strong central government. He felt that by encouraging commercial enterprises, society would be based on earned business success instead of wealth, titles, or land ownership. He believed in taxation to raise money for the government. He wanted to see a trading alliance with Great Britain because it would lead to British investments in U.S. industries. His beliefs would be the basis of the Federalist Party.

Jefferson's Presidency

Jefferson began his presidency by overturning many of the Federalist policies that Adams' administration had put into place. He eliminated domestic taxes, such as the one on whiskey, and cut back on the Treasury Department's attempts to direct the national economy. Jefferson reduced the country's national debt, trimmed back the army, modernized the navy, and established the military academy at West Point, New York.

President Jefferson sent the naval forces to the Mediterranean Sea. Pirates from Tripoli on the North African coast had been attacking U.S. ships for years and holding them for ransom. When the navy arrived, the Pasha of Tripoli declared war on the United States. Battles continued from 1801 to 1805 in what were known as the Barbary Wars. The United States and Tripoli negotiated a peace agreement, and the Mediterranean Sea became safer for ships.

American naval forces battled against pirates in the Barbary Wars.

Jefferson tried to keep the United States from getting involved in foreign wars. When the warring British and French began attacking U.S. ships at sea, Jefferson's solution was the **Embargo** Act of 1807. This act closed U.S. ports to all foreign trade. The embargo was intended to free the United States from European powers, but it crippled the economy by cutting off markets for U.S. goods. The act was repealed by Congress and replaced with a law that restored trade to every nation, except Great Britain and France.

One of Jefferson's greatest contributions as president was the Louisiana Purchase. Jefferson's delegates purchased an enormous piece of land from the French in 1803. They paid $15 million for more than 800,000 square miles of land, doubling the size of the United States.

The Louisiana Purchase 1803

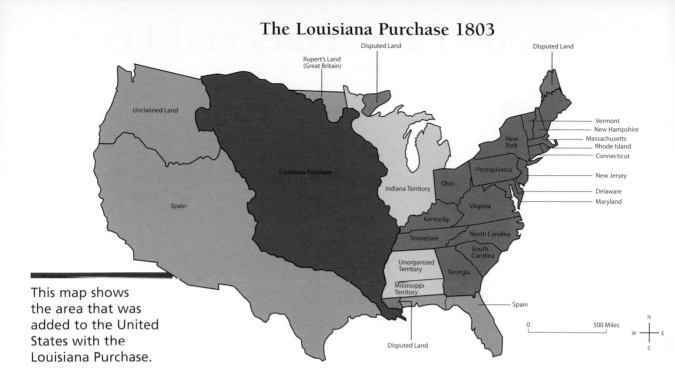

This map shows the area that was added to the United States with the Louisiana Purchase.

At first, Jefferson's Louisiana Purchase was not popular. Since the Constitution had not given the president the right to acquire territory, people were concerned that Jefferson had overstepped his boundaries. The state governments were concerned with the rights that would be given to the people living on the newly-purchased land. Most of the people living on the land did not know it had been sold. Over a period of 80 years, the large territory was integrated into the United States.

Jefferson wanted to know about the land that he had purchased. In 1804, he sent Meriwether Lewis and William Clark to explore the land. The Lewis and Clark expedition traveled all the way from the Mississippi River to the Pacific Ocean and back. They reported on the plants, animals, and people they found. Once

the new territory was explored, Congress established a military government there.

Sacajawea, a young Shoshone Indian, interpreted for Meriwether Lewis and William Clark on their exploration of the West.

Jefferson's Later Years and Legacy

Thomas Jefferson retired to Monticello after his second term as president. He devoted himself to architecture, science, and inventing. Jefferson had a library of thousands of books, known to be the most extensive library in the country. After the British burned the Library of Congress during the War of 1812, Jefferson sold his personal library to Congress as a replacement.

Jefferson founded the University of Virginia in 1819. He was involved in all aspects of creating the new university. Jefferson designed most of the buildings, and he surveyed the campus property. He sent a scout to Great Britain to find professors for the new university.

Jefferson died on July 4, 1826, just a few hours before his friend, John Adams. Jefferson left an enormous legacy for the new United States, both for his role in the American Revolution and his accomplishments as president. Jefferson drafted the Declaration of Independence, which proclaimed the colonies' independence from Great Britain. He was responsible for the Louisiana Purchase, which doubled the size of the United States.

Thomas Jefferson enjoyed architecture. He designed Monticello, his home in Charlottesville, Virginia.

Despite his contributions, Jefferson remains controversial. He was never able to reconcile his thoughts and actions on the subject of slavery. Jefferson wanted the U.S. Constitution to include a section eliminating slavery, but he was a lifelong slave owner. George Washington owned slaves, but freed them upon his death. After Jefferson's death, his slaves were sold to pay his debts. Jefferson felt that slavery was wrong, but he knew that slaves were vital to the plantation economy in which he took part. He struggled with what was right versus what the planters needed.

Jefferson was responsible for some of the basic ideas of American independence. He saw the United States as a great country, populated by people who were all equal. It is still one of the most important visions of the United States.

"Never did a prisoner, released from his chains, feel such relief as I shall on shaking off the shackles of power. Nature intended me for the tranquil pursuits of science, by rendering them my supreme delight. But the enormities of the times in which I have lived, have forced me to... commit myself on the boisterous ocean of political passions."

Thomas Jefferson

George Washington's slaves worked at his Mount Vernon estate. Washington freed his slaves upon his death in 1799.

James Madison's Early Years

James Madison, was born on March 16, 1751, on his family's plantation in Virginia. He came from a wealthy, slave-owning family. During his childhood, Madison played with the children of his family's slaves. Like most boys his age, Madison was educated at home. Later, he was sent to a boarding school and then to the College of New Jersey, which is present-day Princeton University.

Madison was an excellent student, and his greatest interests were history and politics. Madison decided to study law so that he would "depend as little as possible on the labor of slaves."

Madison was a colonel during the the Revolutionary War, but he did not take part in battle. He suffered from poor health his entire life. Madison did take part in the Continental Congress and became good friends with Thomas Jefferson, who at that time was governor of Virginia. Their friendship would last throughout their entire lives.

James Madison was the fourth president of the United States.

Madison is most often remembered as the father of the Constitution because of the role he played in the 1787 Constitutional Convention. Many of his ideas became part of the final constitution. Madison outlined the Virginia Plan, which included a three-part government with separate legislative, executive, and judicial branches.

Madison proposed a system of checks and balances within the government so that one branch could not grow too powerful. Madison kept detailed notes of the entire process of writing the Constitution. He believed it was vital to preserve a record of the process. He wanted other new governments to see how the United States successfully created its constitution.

Early in his political career, Madison's beliefs were similar to those of the Federalists. He had made an extensive study of ancient and modern governments throughout the world. As a result of his work, Madison came to the conclusion that new governments most often failed because they lacked strong central leadership to rule over the individual states or territories within that government. Madison's federalist beliefs, however, would be tested during the presidency of John Adams and would lead to his own terms as president.

DOLLEY MADISON

James Madison's wife, Dolley, was one of the United States most beloved first ladies. Dolley was outgoing and loved to entertain. She presided over official dinners and receptions, first for Thomas Jefferson, who did not have a first lady because of the death of his wife, and then, for her husband. Dolley is best known for her actions during the War of 1812, when the British captured and burned Washington, D.C. She saved many historic paintings and documents from the White House, including a famous painting of George Washington. She escaped just before the British set fire to the building.

James Madison is known as the "Father of the Constitution."

Madison's Early Political Career

Madison played a key role in writing the Constitution and contributed to the process of **ratification**. By ratifying the Constitution, states formally approved the Constitution and agreed to abide by it. Madison, Alexander Hamilton, and John Jay wrote a series of essays called The Federalist Papers in 1787 and 1788. These essays defended the Constitution against its critics and urged its ratification. On June 21, 1788, the Constitution went into effect after being approved by nine states.

In 1788, Madison defeated James Monroe in the first election for the House of Representatives. While serving in the House of Representatives, he helped draft **legislation** to organize the departments of foreign affairs, war, and the treasury. He proposed the Bill of Rights during the first session of Congress in 1789. Madison felt that amendments protecting certain basic rights should be added to the Constitution.

> **"The advice nearest to my heart and deepest in my convictions is that the Union of the States be cherished and perpetuated."**
> *James Madison*

James Madison drafted the Bill of Rights, which protects the basic rights of U.S. citizens. The Bill of Rights was added to the Constitution in 1791.

Madison's estate, Montpelier, was located in Orange, Virginia.

Madison retired from politics in 1797, and returned to his home, Montpelier, in Virginia. He returned to politics because of what he saw as abuses of power by President John Adams and the Federalists. Madison felt that the Alien and Sedition Acts were a disgrace to the ideals of the Constitution. He no longer felt that the country needed a strong central government. Madison and Thomas Jefferson were critical of most of Adams' Federalist policies, and they organized the Democratic-Republican party as an alternative. Known as the Republicans, they believed in stronger roles for the individual states and less power for the federal government.

In 1800, Madison urged his friend Thomas Jefferson to run for president. Jefferson was elected, and he made Madison his secretary of state. Madison defended Jefferson's Louisiana Purchase, as well as the Embargo Act, even though it hurt the United States' economy.

In 1808, Madison ran for president and won by a large majority. He became the fourth president of the United States. As president, he sought to find the balance and restraint that he felt were necessary for a successful government.

THE BILL OF RIGHTS

The Bill of Rights consists of the first 10 amendments to the U.S. Constitution, which protect the rights of individual citizens. These amendments include freedom of religion, freedom of speech, the right to assemble peacefully, the right to bear arms, the right to be protected against unlawful search and seizure, the right to a speedy and public trial for crimes, and the right to a trial by jury. James Madison drafted these amendments to protect civil liberties from the actions of the national government.

Madison's Presidency

The biggest challenge of Madison's presidency was foreign policy. In 1809, Congress repealed the Embargo Act that Jefferson had used as a way to ban trade with other nations that were at war. Congress replaced the act with the Non-Intercourse Act, which banned all trade with Great Britain and France until they stopped interfering with U.S. shipping. Madison received assurances from both countries that they would leave U.S. ships alone, but neither country honored this agreement.

> **"No nation could preserve its freedom in the midst of continual warfare."**
>
> *James Madison*

A faction of Congress known as the "War Hawks" was eager for a war against Great Britain. They wanted the United States to invade Canada as well. The nation was not prepared for war, but Madison gave in to the War Hawks. On June 1, 1812, he asked Congress for a declaration of war. This war became known as the War of 1812.

The United States was unsuccessful early in the war. They were unable to gain territory in Canada, and the British retook most of the Northwest Territories. In 1813, the British blockaded the U.S. coast and prevented ships from sailing. In August 1814, the British marched to Washington, D.C., and burned the Capitol Treasury, the Library of Congress, and the executive mansion, which was later known as the White House.

James Madison served as president from 1809 to 1817.

After the burning of Washington, D.C., the United States had some important military victories. One was the defense of Fort McHenry in Baltimore, Maryland. It was at this battle that Francis Scott Key wrote his poem, "The Star Spangled Banner," which became the national anthem.

In December 1814, British and U.S. diplomats began peace talks in Ghent, Belgium. On Christmas Eve 1814, they signed the Treaty of Ghent, ending the war.

The War of 1812 ended in a stalemate, but it proved to the British that the United States would stand up to them.

It inspired patriotism and unity among the states, as they once again fought a common battle against Great Britain.

Madison finished his terms as president, and he and Dolley returned to Montpelier in 1817. Despite their disagreements, John Adams said of Madison, "Not withstanding a thousand faults and blunders, his administration has acquired more glory and established more Union, than all three of his predecessors... put together."

British soldiers burned books in the Library of Congress and set fire to the building during the War of 1812.

James Monroe's Early Years

James Monroe was the last of the presidents from the Revolutionary War era. He was born on April 28, 1758, in Westmoreland County, Virginia. His family did not have a great deal of money, even though they owned a large plantation.

> "It is particularly gratifying to me to enter on the discharge of these duties at a time when the United States are blessed with peace."
>
> *James Monroe, Inaugural Address, 1817*

James Monroe became the fifth president of the United States.

At 16, Monroe attended the College of William and Mary in Williamsburg, Virginia. He left two years later to fight in the Revolutionary War under General George Washington.

Monroe left the military after the war and studied law under the guidance of Thomas Jefferson, who was then governor of Virginia. In 1784, Monroe met his future wife, Elizabeth Kortright. He and Elizabeth were married in 1786. For the next few years, Monroe was active in Virginia politics. In 1790, he was elected to the U.S. Senate. Like Madison and Jefferson, Monroe opposed the federalist economic ideas of Alexander Hamilton.

In 1794, President Washington appointed James Monroe as a political minister to France. Monroe lived in France during the French Revolution, which he believed was a great war for independence. Washington was concerned that Monroe's sympathy for the French would threaten the United States' position of **neutrality**. Washington called Monroe back to the United States in 1796. Monroe published a defense of his behavior in a book that was also an attack on Federalist foreign policy. Many Republicans agreed with his arguments. From 1799 to 1803, Monroe served as governor of Virginia.

In 1803, President Jefferson sent Monroe on a mission to France to arrange the purchase of New Orleans. Monroe discovered that France was willing to sell even more land, and without permission, he negotiated the Louisiana Purchase. It would add more than 800,000 square miles to the United States.

When James Madison became president in 1811, he appointed Monroe as his secretary of state. During the latter part of the War of 1812, Monroe also acted as secretary of war. He helped keep the British from winning the war and took part in the peace negotiations that brought the war to an end.

Monroe ran for president in 1816 and won by a landslide. Much of Washington, D.C., had been burned by the British, so Monroe delivered his inaugural speech at the Brick Capitol, Congress' temporary meeting hall, in Washington, D.C., Monroe would lead the United States into a time of peace and unity.

THE LOUISIANA PURCHASE.
MESSRS. MONROE AND LIVINGSTONE COMPLETING NEGOTIATIONS WITH TALLYRAND, APRIL 30, 1803

James Monroe helped to negotiate the Louisiana Purchase with France in 1803.

Monroe's Presidency

Four of the first five presidents came from Virginia. James Monroe was the last of this group, which came to be known as the Virginia Dynasty. With the exception of John Adams, the first five presidents were Virginia planters who felt that their positions made them best-suited for political office. These first presidents were participants in the Revolutionary War. They had been chiefly concerned with building and defending their new nation. Monroe would be the first to focus on expanding the nation and giving it a presence in the world.

In 1819, Monroe acquired Florida from the Spanish, as well as all former Spanish claims to the Oregon Territory in the Adams-Onís Treaty. Monroe contested Russia's claim to the west coast of America. Eventually Russia was restricted to what is now Alaska, and even this claim would end in 1867, when the United States acquired that territory.

In 1823, Monroe presented Congress with the Monroe Doctrine. With the help of his secretary of state, John Quincy Adams, Monroe stated that the American continent would no longer be considered as a place for foreign countries to colonize. The Monroe Doctrine was issued in response to continued threats from Europe to reclaim former lands in the United States. It would protect the new independence of Latin American nations and prevent European influence there.

The doctrine stated that the United States would not interfere in European affairs

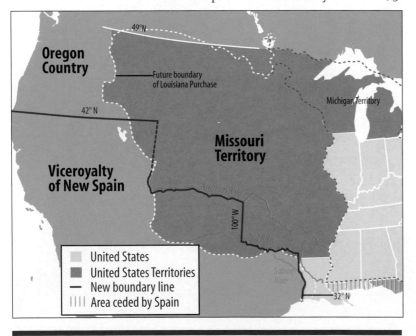

This map shows the area that the United States acquired from Spain in the Adams-Onís Treaty.

President Monroe discussed the Monroe Doctrine with his advisors, especially his secretary of state, John Quincy Adams.

unless they were protecting their own interests. The Monroe Doctrine was the United States' declaration that it was now a major world power. It would guide U.S. foreign policy for many years. The Monroe Doctrine was one of Monroe's greatest achievements.

President Monroe also made progress in domestic affairs. He reduced taxes and paid off much of the government's debt. In 1820, he signed the Missouri Compromise, which forbid slavery in the Louisiana Territory above the southern border of Missouri. This temporarily kept the peace between states that allowed slavery and states that did not. It did not solve the problem of slavery, but it was a compromise until a more permanent solution could be found. President Monroe's action kept the country together for another 40 years until the outbreak of the Civil War in 1861.

James Monroe retired in 1825, after two terms as president. He went on to act as regent of the University of Virginia. He presided over the Virginia state constitutional convention in 1829. Monroe died on July 4, 1831, in New York City.

"ERA OF GOOD FEELINGS"

James Monroe's presidency is often referred to as the "Era of Good Feelings." This was a brief period of time when the Republicans were virtually unopposed. A newspaper reporter in Boston coined the phrase The Era of Good Feelings to describe the lack of party conflict. Also contributing was the unity and patriotism inspired by the War of 1812. The United States was finding its identity, and instead of being "New Yorkers" or "Virginians," people began thinking of themselves as "Americans."

Monroe's Legacy

James Monroe was the last of the Revolutionary War presidents and the first to focus on expansion. By asserting the United States' right not to be invaded or colonized, he made other countries see the nation as a world power. His Monroe Doctrine would guide the nation's foreign policy for many years.

Monroe is also remembered for committing his administration to expanding the country's system of roads and canals. With the difficulties of moving troops and supplies during the War of 1812, and the expansion of the country, the nation needed a better system of transportation. This concern with transportation led to the construction of the Erie Canal.

Towns quickly sprang up along the Erie Canal.

Begun in 1817, the Erie Canal it was a man-made waterway that flowed 363 miles from the Hudson River to Lake Erie. Until the construction of railroads, it was one of the United States' most important methods of transportation.

Madison created the National Road, which stretched from Maryland to Virginia. Smaller roads branched off the National Road, creating a road system around every major city.

Madison held the United States together at a time when the issue of slavery was beginning to divide the North and the South. Although his Missouri Compromise was just that, a compromise, it would give the United States 40 more years before the Civil War nearly ended the Union.

Monroe restored peace and prosperity to the United States after the War of 1812. His presidency successfully spanned the transition from the United States as a new nation to the age of expansion and reform.

> **"Monroe was so honest that if you turned his soul inside out there would not be a spot on it."**
>
> *Thomas Jefferson*

President Monroe is best known for his Monroe Doctrine, which forbid European countries from intervening in the Western Hemisphere.

Timeline

The years of 1750 to 1800 saw the creation of a new, independent nation. The 13 original colonies declared their independence from Great Britain and created a new nation, the United States of America. It took the careful guidance of the first five presidents to make this a successful transition. Not only did they have to fight for their independence during the Revolutionary War, but take the

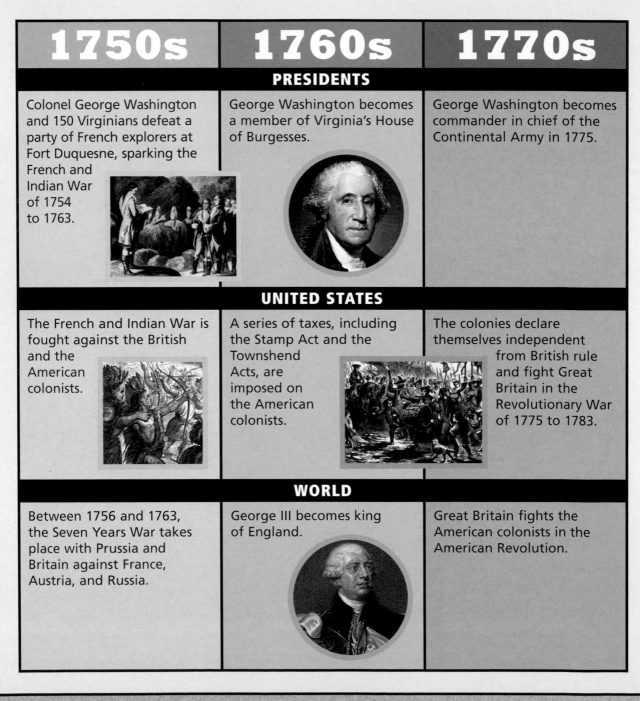

1750s	1760s	1770s
PRESIDENTS		
Colonel George Washington and 150 Virginians defeat a party of French explorers at Fort Duquesne, sparking the French and Indian War of 1754 to 1763.	George Washington becomes a member of Virginia's House of Burgesses.	George Washington becomes commander in chief of the Continental Army in 1775.
UNITED STATES		
The French and Indian War is fought against the British and the American colonists.	A series of taxes, including the Stamp Act and the Townshend Acts, are imposed on the American colonists.	The colonies declare themselves independent from British rule and fight Great Britain in the Revolutionary War of 1775 to 1783.
WORLD		
Between 1756 and 1763, the Seven Years War takes place with Prussia and Britain against France, Austria, and Russia.	George III becomes king of England.	Great Britain fights the American colonists in the American Revolution.

ideals of the new nation and form a strong government. As a result of the work of Washington, Adams, Jefferson, Madison, and Monroe, the country moved from being an infant nation to an acknowledged member of the world community. These five presidents paved the way for the United States to move ahead and focus on itself. After 50 years of work toward becoming a nation, it was time to concentrate on expansion, as well as reforming parts of the government that were not working.

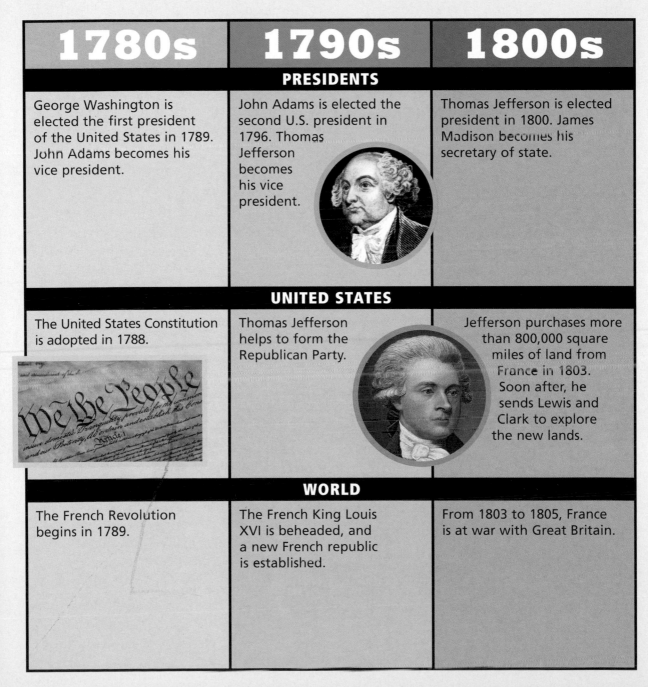

1780s	1790s	1800s
PRESIDENTS		
George Washington is elected the first president of the United States in 1789. John Adams becomes his vice president.	John Adams is elected the second U.S. president in 1796. Thomas Jefferson becomes his vice president.	Thomas Jefferson is elected president in 1800. James Madison becomes his secretary of state.
UNITED STATES		
The United States Constitution is adopted in 1788.	Thomas Jefferson helps to form the Republican Party.	Jefferson purchases more than 800,000 square miles of land from France in 1803. Soon after, he sends Lewis and Clark to explore the new lands.
WORLD		
The French Revolution begins in 1789.	The French King Louis XVI is beheaded, and a new French republic is established.	From 1803 to 1805, France is at war with Great Britain.

Activity

During the first years of the newly formed United States, there were many differences in political opinions as to the role of the federal government. The Federalists wanted a strong central government, while the Democratic-Republicans thought that the government's power should center more on the states and individual citizens. This difference in political opinion still exists in the modern Republican and Democratic parties.

Decide if you agree with the Federalists or the Democratic-Republicans. Based on what you have learned about these two groups and their different approaches to government, imagine that it is just after the American Revolution and you are in charge of establishing the new government. Set up a plan for the central government according to how your political group feels it should be run. Consider these questions. Should there be a president? If not, who or what will lead the country? If so, how much power should the president have? Should there be a government with three branches? Will any one part of the government be stronger than the others? How much authority should the central government have over the states?

Then, present your plan for this new government to your friends. They can vote to decide which government sounds like the best choice for a new nation.

Quiz

1. True or False? The Declaration of Independence was written in 1776.

2. What was the name of George Washington's home in Virginia?
   A. Mount Vernon
   B. Monticello
   C. Montpelier

3. Whose son served as the sixth president?
   A. George Washington
   B. John Adams
   C. Thomas Jefferson

4. Who saved historic documents from the White House before it burned?
   A. George Washington
   B. Dolley Madison
   C. Martha Washington

5. True or False? Jefferson sent Meriwether Lewis and William Clark to explore the Louisiana Purchase.

6. True or False? Monroe was the last president of the Virginia Dynasty.

7. True or False? Thomas Jefferson served as a diplomat to Germany.

8. James Madison attended which college?
   A. Harvard College
   B. College of William and Mary
   C. The College of New Jersey

9. Monroe's expansion of the transportation system led to the construction of:
   A. the Erie Canal.
   B. the Transcontinental Railroad.
   C. Robert Fulton's steamboat.

Answers 1. True 2. A 3. B 4. B 5. True 6. True 7. False. Thomas Jefferson served as a diplomat to France. 8. C 9. A

Further Research

Books

To find out more about U.S. presidents, visit your local library. Most libraries have computers that connect to a database for researching information. If you enter a keyword, you will be provided with a list of books in the library that contain information on that topic. Non-fiction books are arranged numerically, using their call number. Fiction books are organized alphabetically by the author's last name.

Websites

The World Wide Web is a good source of information. Reputable websites usually include government sites, educational sites, and online encyclopedias. Visit the following sites to learn more about U.S. presidents.

The official White House website offers a short history of the U.S. presidency, along with biographical sketches and portraits of all the presidents to date. **www.whitehouse.gov/history/presidents**

This website contains background information, election results, cabinet members, and notable events for each of the presidents. **www.ipl.org/div/potus**

Explore the lives and careers of every U.S. president on the PBS website. **www.pbs.org/wgbh/amex/presidents**

Glossary

amendments: revisions or changes made to a law, bill, or document

cabinet: a group of men who advise the president

controversial: something that may create arguments or disagreements

delegates: official representatives to a conference or large political gathering

democracy: a government run by the people through their elected representatives

disbanded: when a group or organization is broken up

embargo: a government order forbidding foreign ships from entering or leaving its ports

inauguration: a ceremony that takes place when a new president takes office

legislation: a law or bill being considered by a legislative group

militia: a group of citizens who can be called for military service in an emergency

negotiate: to discuss or bargain in order to reach an agreement

neutrality: the position of not taking sides while other nations are fighting

precedents: rules or actions that will be an example for similar future situations

ratification: to formally confirm or approve something such as a treaty or a constitution

repealed: canceled or changed a decision or a law

treaty: a formal, signed agreement between states or countries

unconstitutional: something that does not follow the rules of the Constitution

Index